Nature Upclose

A Mouse's Life

Written and Illustrated by John Himmelman

Children's Press®
A Division of Grolier Publishing

New York London Hong Kong Sydney
Danbury, Connecticut

For Mon, who LOVES the little mice!

Library of Congress Cataloging-in-Publication Data

Himmelman, John
   A mouse's life / written and illustrated by John Himmelman.
      p. cm. — (Nature upclose)
   Summary: Describes the daily activities and life cycle of a
white-footed mouse.
   ISBN 0-516-21167-6 (lib. bdg.)   0-516-27287-X (pbk.)
   1. Peromyscus—Juvenile literature. [1. White-footed mouse.
2. Mice.] I. Title. II. Series.
QL737.R666 H56 2000
599.35'5—dc21

                                     00-27012

Visit Children's Press® on the Internet at:
  http://publishing.grolier.com

White-footed Mouse
Peromyscus leucopsus

The white-footed mouse is common through-out most of the United States and Canada. It usually sleeps during the day and spends the night searching for food. Seeds and nuts are this mouse's favorite food, but it also eats insects, fruit, and mushrooms. Of course, a piece of cheese left out is always welcome.

    The white-footed mouse is active all year long. It builds a nest of twigs, leaves, and grass in tree holes, abandoned bird houses, wood piles. It may even make a nest in your attic or basement.

    Owls and cats are the biggest enemies of the white-footed mouse. When a mouse senses danger, it drums its feet to warn other mice. Then, the mice run and hide until the danger has passed.

    White-footed mice live for about 2 to 3 years in the wild. They may give birth as many as four times a year. Each litter has two to six babies. That's a lot of mice!

On a warm summer morning, a female white-footed mouse
gives birth to three tiny babies.

The mice grow quickly. Soon, they open their eyes and grow a coat of fur.

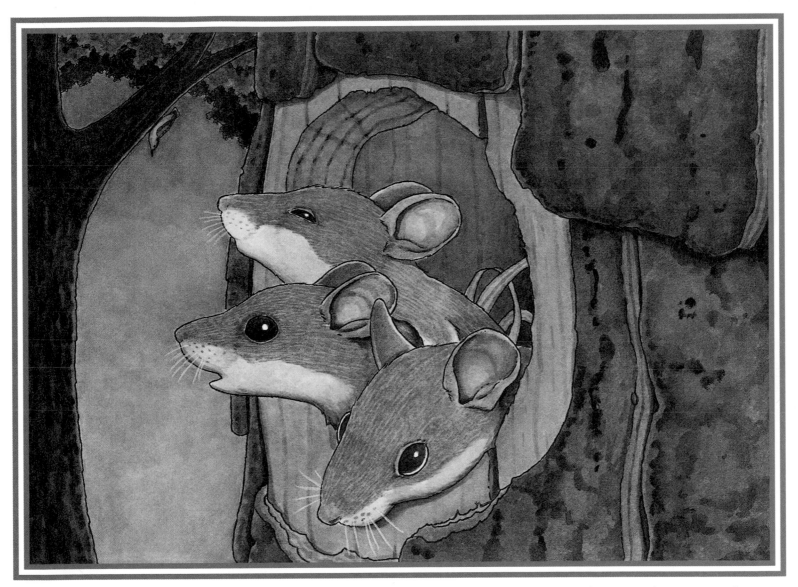

After just a few weeks, the young mice are ready to leave their nest.

When night comes, one of the mice scampers down the tree.

He finds a cherry on the ground and takes a few bites.

The mouse tries to eat a *katydid*, but it is too big.

All through the summer, the mouse spends his nights searching for food. After about 6 weeks, he is full grown.

One night, a dark shadow suddenly blocks the moonlight.

A *barn owl* swoops down to catch the mouse!

The mouse dives under a log. This time he is safe.

Soon, the days grow chilly. The mouse looks for a warm place to spend the winter.

He finds an empty bird house and builds a nest inside.

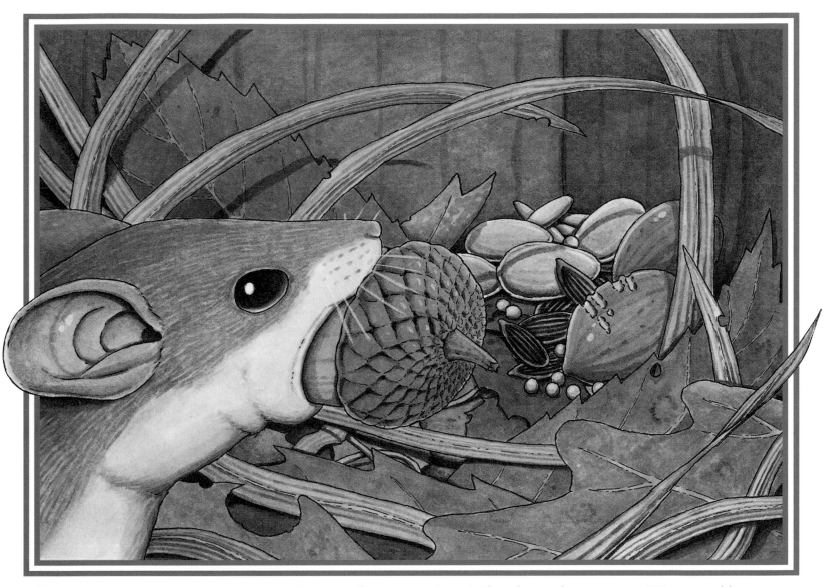

The mouse stores seeds and nuts inside his house. He will eat them during the winter.

The mouse stays busy all winter long.

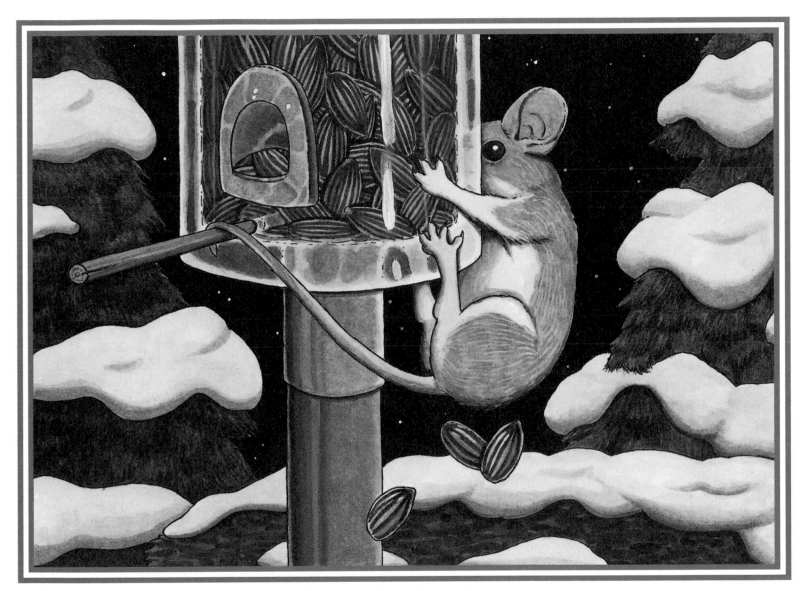

He spends his nights looking for food.

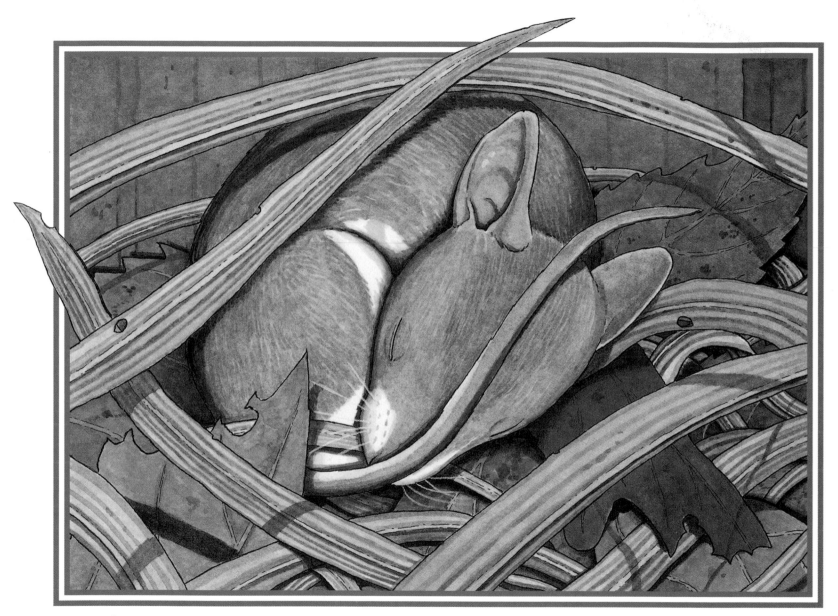

He sleeps in his nest during the day.

When spring arrives, the white-footed mouse finds a female.

After the mice mate, the male leaves. The female will take care of the young by herself.

The male mouse is thirsty. He finds a small puddle and takes a long drink.

The mouse doesn't know he is in danger. A hungry cat grabs him . . .

. . . and carries him into a house!

A child rescues the mouse and puts him in a jar. The child gives him peanuts.

In the morning, the child lets the mouse go free.

The mouse heads back to his home.

But a *bluebird* has taken over his nest!

The mouse makes a new nest under a *brush pile*.

For the rest of his life, the mouse spends his days sleeping in a warm nest.

At night, he hunts for food and escapes from enemies.

Words You Know

barn owl—a large bird with a white, heart-shaped face. A barn owl may eat as many as three mice a night and more than 1,000 mice a year.

bluebird—a small bird with blue feathers that sings a beautiful song. It eats insects, spiders, and berries.

brush pile—a large bunch of tree branches on the ground

katydid—a bright green grasshopper-like insect with long antennae. A male katydid can make music by rubbing his wings together.

About the Author

John Himmelman is a naturalist who enjoys turning over dead logs, crawling through grass, kneeling over puddles, and gazing at the sky. His greatest joy is sharing these experiences with others. He has written or illustrated more than fifty books for children, including *Ibis: A True Whale Story, Wanted: Perfect Parents*, and *J.J. Versus the Babysitter*.

His books have received honors, such as CBC/NSTA Outstanding Science Trade Book for Children, Pick of the List, Book of the Month, JLG Selection, and the ABC Award. Some of the illustrations he has created for the Nature Upclose series were featured at an exhibit at Yale University's Peabody Museum of Natural History. John lives in Killingworth, Connecticut, with his wife, Betsy, who is an art teacher. They have two children, Jeff and Liz.